DYNAMICS
of SPIRITUAL
DECEPTION

Daniel C. Juster, Th.D.

WESTBOW
PRESS®
A DIVISION OF THOMAS NELSON
& ZONDERVAN

WestBow Press books may be ordered through booksellers or by contacting:

WestBow Press
A Division of Thomas Nelson & Zondervan
1663 Liberty Drive
Bloomington, IN 47403
www.westbowpress.com
1 (866) 928-1240

ISBN: 978-1-5127-2242-0 (sc)
ISBN: 978-1-5127-2241-3 (e)

Library of Congress Control Number: 2015919955

Print information available on the last page.

WestBow Press rev. date: 1/18/2016

CONTENTS

DEDICATION

To the late Chaplain Dr. Evan D. Welsh and Mrs. Evan (Oleina May) Welsh. Their spiritual life and love gave an image of truth which kept us during difficult years.

PREFACE

Forty-five years ago my wife and I were part of a congregation that fell into depths of spiritual deception and became cultic. The events of those days led to the ruin of many lives. Most shocking of all was the number of students from Evangelical backgrounds who were so easily deceived. How did this happen? What were the spiritual principles involved which led to such a great tragedy?

It is my conviction that the account of this congregation and the review of the principles involved in their deception will prevent the same thing from occurring elsewhere. May those who read this learn to guard themselves against the dynamics of spiritual deception.

Due to the sensitive nature of this story, names and places have been altered. However the substance of this account is true.

More than 20 years have passed since this book was first published. It still amazes me that this book still describes parallels to so many situations today. I trust that the reading of this book will prevent some from entering into the deceptions described and that others will be more fully healed.

THE STORY OF DECEPTION

We sat in a circle, sang lively choruses, and clapped our hands. Then we stood in reverence and sang worship choruses. The words were sung with great feeling and awe: "Bless the LORD, O my soul, and all that is within me bless His holy name." Some eyes were closed, while others reflected the presence of tears. Hands were raised in adoration, and as the chorus came to an end, many began to sing in hushed tones of strange syllables. It was a peculiar harmony, like that of an Aeolian harp, and it had an eerie beauty. This was followed by silence, until one man across this circle of 25 to 35 people began to speak out loud in strange syllables:

"Shobo-to ka a be, shodo-ma sondanai, kobakai
lodo-ma kambi, shotoma kandi, tobatai shobo-to
kabe, kobakai, sundakai."[1]

---

[1] Although this is not the exact speech, it is a reasonable approximation of the sound from this man, heard many times over two years.

Silence followed. Then an attractive short-haired girl whom I had not yet met said, "I love you, my people. Abide in me forever. I love you and give you life."

Then others spoke. Some read Scripture. Others gave words as if God were speaking through them in the first person:

> "My children, I desire to dwell in your midst. Yield yourselves wholly to Me; then I will fill you. You cannot do it, but only by My living My life through you – thus saith the LORD."

Several others spoke in a similar vein. My mind was racing, why did so many speak in King James Elizabethan English? Was this really the Word of the LORD? Were these the gifts of the Spirit? Was I in the midst of the supernatural presence of God? Was this group returning to a real New Testament expression of the power and presence of God?

But the biggest question of all was, "What was I doing at Flock Church?" This was not my first experience with "Charismatics" or "Pentecostal Christians." Nor was I ignorant of their doctrine. I began to look back over my life to discover what had led me there.

<u>Personal History</u>

Because my father was Jewish and my mother a Norwegian Christian, I was not raised in either a Christian community or a synagogue. My father died as I approached my ninth birthday.

One morning as I was shooting baskets in the local outdoor court in River Edge, New Jersey, I had a deep sense of God speaking to me. I did not hear an audible voice, but rather I had an intuitive perception of Him speaking to me. The message was that I should be relating to Him. "How do I relate to God?" I wondered. Then a thought came to me: I should go to a Christian church or a synagogue.

I had cousins whom I liked very much on my mother's side. They always went to Sunday school and a Christian church. One Sunday I decided to join them. It was a lively congregation under Evangelical Reformed Church of America. It was there that I heard the Gospel for the first time and decided to make a commitment to the LORD as a result of the inspiring sermon by the guest speaker George Sweeting.

Soon afterward I decided to go to the Word of Life Camp. There, at the age of 12, I dedicated my life to the LORD. Indeed, I became very committed and very involved during my high school years. I attended Sunday school and services on Sunday mornings, youth groups and evening services on Sunday nights, and a high school Bible club on Monday nights. I spent six summers at Word of Life Camp – first as a camper, then as a counselor in training, and finally as a counselor.

Gradually a desire grew in me to know the LORD well, to walk in close fellowship with Him, and eventually to become a pastor. How my heart burned during great preaching! In high school I was known as "the preacher." With God's help I went from an obese 278 pounds to a rail at 162 pounds. Those were good years, full of purpose and joy. There were times of backsliding, but in general I lived as a Christian. I loved this congregation; I would cry during the singing of great hymns and recite the Apostle's Creed[2] with joy and confidence.

It was during these years that I first became acquainted with Charismatics. One was Larry Carroll, a saintly elder in the Reformed Church; the other was Judy, the female youth director. They introduced me to the writings of Andrew Murray and Watchman Nee and spoke of the deeper spiritual life available through the "baptism in the Holy Spirit." I longed for this experience, and finally I asked them to come lay their hands on me. There was a sense that I had received this baptism in the Holy

---

[2]   Ancient statement of faith

Spirit – a release; so we praised God. Although they both spoke in tongues, I did not have the experience at that time. However, they assured me that I had the baptism in the Holy Spirit by faith, even if I did not speak in tongues.

Great joy followed for many weeks. Bible studies for young people at the home of Larry Carroll were filled with great spiritual fervor and depth. However, I still loved the anti-charismatic Word of Life Camp and never separated from other Christians on the basis of this experience. Some left our congregation because it was not "Spirit-filled," but I loved our congregation.

Two other experiences influenced me and are worth noting. One was a visit to Teen Challenge in New York City after reading *The Cross and the Switchblade* by David Wilkerson. Although they clapped and sang with fervor, there was no special manifestation. The other event was a visit to a Bible study in Manhattan held in the home of John McCandlish Phillips, the award-winning New York Times writer. The "Yale God Squad" (a group of Yale students who were known for bold witnessing) attended these meetings. The study was interesting, and the atmosphere was warm. There was prophecy of a limited nature, but I did not know what to make of it.

After graduation from high school in 1965, I decided to attend the King's College in Westchester County, New York. This was to prepare for an eventual seminary education. King's is a soundly Evangelical college. I thoroughly enjoyed my freshman year, went to summer school, and looked forward to my sophomore year. As a sophomore, I found a new girlfriend. Also, I was involved in many extra-curricular activities, including ministerial club, foreign missions club, prayer meetings, and the King's Club visitation team which visited homes for the elderly. Included as well was a heavy academic schedule. I bragged that I only needed four hours of sleep a night – that the LORD was my strength. Then the bottom fell out!

I had thought that my girlfriend was to become my wife and that God had shown by many circumstances that she was "the one!" In getting to know her better, I discovered a deep melancholy which had been hidden underneath an external projection of happiness. Since I was only 19 years old, I found her depressions frightening.

At the same time that I was going through this emotional turmoil, I was also studying the history of philosophy. A question loomed in my mind. Why should I consider Christianity to be true when there are scores of competing world views in the history of philosophy? Why Christianity rather than Hegel, Shopenhauer, or Spinoza? Why not Hinduism? The questions were suppressed until one morning I awoke with a feeling of dread.

I was exhausted and full of guilt and skepticism concerning the truth of Christianity. I was afraid to live and afraid to die. My good friend and roommate Roy Sutten, who had experienced his own trauma, was aware of my state. He knew I was living on a treadmill leading to a crash, but I refused to listen to his advice. After accepting only his empathy, I drove home for Thanksgiving break.

I was in a terrible state. My mother was so alarmed that she took me to our family physician who prescribed rest and gave me antidepressants.

The rest of that year was characterized by fear, depression and skepticism. I commuted to college from home and took fewer courses. Dr. Daniels, a Christian psychiatrist, was a good friend and confidant during those troubled times. He radiated love and patience in his counseling. However, few others seemed to understand my depression. It was not until years later that a firm faith was reestablished.

Because I saw myself becoming too dependent by living at home – and because I wanted to study apologetics, philosophy and world religions on the highest academic level possible – I decided to transfer to Wheaton College in Illinois. My application was accepted and, despite my fears of leaving home, I made the final decision to go.

It was hard to bid farewell to my best friends Ed Demarest, Roy Sutten, and especially to Mom. Leaving the psychiatrist was frightening, too. However, I was convinced I had to take that step to keep myself from becoming a dependent vegetable.

Mom and I drove to Wheaton, and I settled into the new men's dorm. The next day, after driving Mom to the airport, the dread and fear returned. I felt lonely and abandoned and desperately needed some evidence that there was a purpose to the world and a meaning to life.

Someone recommended going to see Chaplain Welsh. He was a saintly man in his sixties, full of love and warmth. His counsel, his love, and the openness of his home became to me a sustaining source of life. He was the most important influence in my return to faith, even though that return was still some years away.

Introduction to Flock Church

While I plunged into classes and the usual collegiate activities, I also heard about a group on campus that gathered for "charismatic worship." They claimed some real miracles. Perhaps this would reveal new evidence of the reality of God. Some of the students in this group were also beginning to attend a congregation in which the pastor had just received the baptism in the Holy Spirit. This was a mainline denominational congregation attended by many prominent members of a suburban community some 25 minutes from Wheaton. I decided to investigate.

Several events convinced me to attend this congregation. One was a tape played in a Sociology of Religion class. It presented the reality of the Holy Spirit; the teacher on the tape was Kevin Ranigan, the well-known Catholic charismatic theologian. I learned that my sociology teacher believed the message of the tape and was going to be attending this congregation, Flock Church.

The second event was a chapel talk on the Holy Spirit. Two Wheaton professors presented their views along with the pastor of Flock Church. He testified powerfully on the reality of the gifts of the Holy Spirit and of the manifestations of bona fide supernatural gifts in his congregation. It was very impressive.

The following weekend two nursing students from Wheaton's West Suburban Nursing School arranged to go on a date with me and Jerry, another Wheaton student whom I had not met before. After we dropped the girls off, Jerry and I remained together discussing many topics. I mentioned my faith struggles and my interest in attending Flock Church. Jerry excitedly replied that he had recently received the baptism in the Holy Spirit. We made arrangements to go together.

Sunday morning was a momentous day at Flock Church. The service was relatively similar to most mainline congregations. However, when the time came to baptize infants, the pastor announced that he could not in good conscience carry out this part of the service. He then gave a sermon in which he explained his new convictions concerning "believer's baptism," linking it to the new move of the Holy Spirit in the congregation. From then on, Sunday morning would never be the same. The gifts of the Spirit would be allowed to flow and only adult believers' baptism by immersion would be practiced. For many old-time members, this marked their last service at Flock Church.

No manifestations of a supernatural character took place at this service. Even so, I was impressed by the courage of Pastor Tabor, especially after I later learned that his stand had cost him about half of his congregation. Previous to his Holy Spirit experience, he had been a typical social-activist, mainline-type pastor. After his experience with a local charismatic Episcopal priest, he was ready to turn his congregation upside down.

Pastor Tabor was a strange man. A combination of shyness and bluntness paradoxically characterized both his public and personal conversation. It was disarming, to say the least. Though I never quite gained an intimate personal understanding of him, a general understanding did develop. I decided I would return to Flock for the Sunday evening service and see if there was a real evidence of the supernatural for apologetic purposes.

I experienced this season with Pastor Tabor during the rebellious era of the Vietnam War. Protests and debates were prominent at Wheaton. The old value system seemed to be destined for a major overhaul, or at least a revision. Even Wheaton College could not escape the effects of the 1960's. In this context, I found myself sitting in this small circle listening to the prophecies, prayers, Scriptures, and Pastor Tabor's rambling messages. Pastor Tabor always gave rambling messages, but they were filled with words of faith and the power of God.

I attended both this congregation and the campus prayer group for Charismatics. The worship at Flock was unlike anything I had ever experienced before. There was an outpouring of fervent devotion, a joy, a release in the Spirit, and spontaneity; yet I was in many ways a bystander, a neutral observer. I had not yet found my "objective" proof of the reality of it all. Perhaps, in Orwell's terms, it was only "group-think." Perhaps it was only a reflection of the emotionalism of "true believers." Most of the miracles seemed quite minor and amenable to other explanations. Headaches, colds, and nebulous pains were cured – but not heart disease, cancer, or atrophied limbs. Yet I continued to attend, hoping perhaps to see the angel of Bethesda stir the waters and produce a bona fide miracle, inexplicable by known natural causes. I even sometimes thought I sensed a presence of God in these services, though I would later discount it. What an amazing thing it was to sing,

> "Let all that is within me cry, 'Holy, holy is the Lamb that was slain!'" and "Thou art worthy to receive glory, honor, and power."

So I continued to attend the congregation and to study philosophy, hoping for evidence from some sphere. Chaplain Welsh provided comfort, while my professors provided direction for study. The three most influential were brilliant philosophy teachers: David Wolfe, now of Gordon College, Stuart Hackett of Trinity Divinity School, and Arthur Holmes of Wheaton College.

GROWTH AT FLOCK

Then the congregation underwent *significant* change. First of all, the professor who led the campus group for Charismatics urged his group to attend Flock. This brought a noticeable addition of students. These students in turn invited others. Though students from other colleges also came, Wheaton predominated. Secondly, committed older members invited friends and relatives. Many were saved. Thirdly, several key professors joined: a sociologist, a philosopher, and a communications teacher, all from Wheaton. Indeed, the congregation was growing. Within a few months all previous membership losses were recovered. The worship was better than ever. Guest preachers such as Ern Baxter provided magnificent preaching, and Pastor Tabor continued his rambling sermons.

Flock Church was part of the early charismatic renewal outside of Pentecostalism. Although I could not yet prove the supernatural from personal experience, I was attracted by the vibrant, joyous, and reverent worship. During this period, members were encouraged to absorb the teachings of James Beall of Detroit, Derek Prince, Ern Baxter, and Harry Greenwood.

SPEAKING IN TONGUES

As the Christmas holiday approached, the congregation was packed one night. The worship was glorious, and even the message was better than usual. I decided to speak to the pastor after the service concerning my spiritual battles. Perhaps he could add some new light.

Jerry came with me into the pastor's study. I explained my problem, and Pastor Tabor replied, "Your problem is that you need the baptism in the Holy Spirit." Well, perhaps so. Maybe it would be so directly supernatural that my doubts would be gone. Therefore I submitted to the laying on of hands. As they prayed in tongues and urged me to join in, I found myself speaking forth a torrent of new unlearned syllables. Indeed, we prayed and sang in tongues for quite a while. Jerry was ecstatic. He even prayed that the nature of the tongue might change. He professed that as he prayed, my syllables changed to a different type of language.

What was this experience? Was it a real language? Was it proof of God? The questions raced through my mind, but I felt it better not to discuss them with my ecstatic friend Jerry. All during the Christmas break, I continued to speak in tongues while still raising the same questions. Indeed, I later found many books and articles explaining what was called "glossolalia" from many different perspectives. Some explained it psychologically, others anthropologically. Some claimed it was a real language, while others said it was nonsense. Still others held it to be a linguistic expression with some of the characteristics of a real language, but without other characteristics. What confusion!

EARLY TIMES AT FLOCK

Nevertheless, I returned to my studies at Wheaton to seek rational-empirical evidence for meaning and purpose while still attending Flock Church to look for a true miracle. This was a very significant period for me because I was intensely studying eastern religious philosophy. My critical abilities began to gel as I read theology, philosophy, and Christian history with greater ease and understanding. The ability to compare and contrast viewpoints was crucial in evaluating the next eighteen months.

At Wheaton, I met a new friend in the oratorio choir just before Christmas break. His name was Jack Colpepper. Jack was of Mennonite extraction and the son of a deceased Baptist minister. He was a very lovable person with a warm ear-to-ear smile. One day I mentioned to him that I was looking for a new roommate. "So am I," he blurted out. We therefore decided to room together.

Also during this time, I was developing a relationship with the charismatic philosophy professor who attended Flock. He encouraged me to take a more existential approach to events and to recognize that knowledge is derived from faith. Dr. Ziegler was a warm and accepting person, but I had difficulty with his "faith-approach" to these significant questions. I identified with the hard-nosed rational approach of Dr. Hackett, professor of Philosophy of Religion.

One day, soon after Jack and I became roommates, I invited Jack to accompany me to Flock Church. "Perhaps you could give me your opinion; it might be helpful," I added.

When the service was over, I asked for his opinion. He said, "This is the New Testament church!" Jack proceeded to become an ardent member of the congregation, and other friends followed. I desired to participate fully but could not seem to lose my objective distance from it all.

Our group of friends consisted of Bill, a brilliant young man who was training to be a European missionary, his girlfriend Janice, and Jerry's new girlfriend Mary. We were a unique group. Sometimes my friends bore with me; other times they chastised me. At worst they avoided me. However, they were my college friends.

So the year continued. Studies progressed. The true miracle did not occur. Summer vacation came.

UNHEALTHY SHIFT

The following fall I picked up where I had left off, and this was during a year of great transition in the congregation. There were new phenomena such as directive prophecy and various thrusts in evangelism. However, the greatest shift was a slow but steady progress in the congregation toward a new and bizarre understanding of the Scripture and the proper approach to it.

There was a good service one particular October evening. I remember it well. Pastor Tabor gave an unusually coherent message. And afterward I complimented him on it. "Did you receive it with your intellect or with your spirit?" he replied.

I answered, "With both."

This incident is an illustration of a gradual turn to new attitudes and perspectives. A great emphasis was placed on the pride of the intellect. The intellect was considered a barrier to true spiritual understanding. The pastor and many of the students spoke of Evangelicalism as a dead, intellectual faith. A sharp demarcation was made between "Spirit-filled" Christians and "non-Spirit-filled." This seemed ludicrous to me, since some very immature people described themselves as "Spirit-filled," while they would say of Chaplain Welsh, for example, that he was not Spirit-filled.

I questioned, "How can a saintly, loving, and kind person who gives testimony of many spiritual experiences of a supernatural kind not be Spirit-filled, while these immature folks who speak in tongues are Spirit-filled? Can we really make these synonymous?"

When I raised these questions with my circle of friends, I was told that the problem was my intellect. I now realize that there *is* a pride of the intellect that is a great barrier to receiving spiritual truth. Yet, do we not need to weigh the issues of evidence and truth in the mind? I wrestled with a slow but definite development of an anti-intellectual tone that began to grow at Flock Church.

BAPTISM

The preaching that fall began to emphasize Romans 6. This passage, on our co-death and resurrection with Jesus, was tied very closely to a new emphasis on baptism. There was a great emphasis on the need for all to be fully immersed in the *name of Jesus* for the specific cutting off of the old person. It was emphasized that baptism was a *real work*, a necessity to complete the salvation experience. Prophetic words confirmed this message.

That same fall I met my future wife. She was related to another Flock member in our circle of friendship. We would all discuss the teaching and prophecy coming forth at the congregation. Soon, most of us were convinced of the need to be re-baptized. Some had never been immersed – including myself. Scripturally, it was something I sensed I should do to ensure that I had fully obeyed all of Scripture. Along with my girlfriend Patty and several friends, we were baptized or re-baptized by Pastor Tabor. In our case, I thought, perhaps we would be given greater faith-ability through this action.

It was a glorious service at the rented facilities of the local Baptist congregation. The singing was exuberant, and the testimonies were exciting. The response of applause and joy for each baptized person was a shout of victory. How well I remember the people that night! There was my roommate Jack, his great smile beaming, along with the quiet, joyous look of the sociology professor. Nearby sat Jerry and Mary. Mary had originally fled in terror from the manifestations of the campus prayer meeting. Now, however, she was convinced by both Jerry and her own searching that this was right. They looked at me with an expression which said, "Now you will finally be truly one with us."

Also present were Bill, our suite-mate, and his girlfriend Janice, a tall and exuberant girl from a Pentecostal background. Bill kept telling me I had a skeptical mindset, not intellectual problems with the faith. Janice spoke of her personal experience with the power of God. How I loved them all – such good people! Yet how the doubts still lingered!

TENSION GROWS

Patty and I continued to share our burdens with Chaplain Welsh. He provided warmth, spoke well of those who claimed he was not Spirit-filled, and gave us hope and affirmation. Additionally, that fall I had become the assistant in Philosophy of Religion to Dr. Stuart Hackett, a brilliant lecturer with a classical Thomistic perspective.

The dichotomy was a real tension. Flock was tainted with anti-intellectualism, but my course of study and my responsibilities were highly intellectual. However, the anti-intellectualism was not yet that severe. In fact, the intellectual members interpreted the anti-intellectual bias to be more an expression against false rationalistic approaches in thinking and not opposed to the proper use of the intellect. Therefore, I hoped that greater balance and clarity would come and the tension would be lessened.

Later that fall, several of the Flock students of Wheaton had prophetic words of a directive nature within their prayer groups. One led to my roommate Jack dating an attractive, bright-eyed, enthusiastic girl named Susan. Another word confirmed the marriage of Jerry and Mary.

Jerry was a junior and Mary was a sophomore. Mary's parents were against the marriage, but they acquiesced when Mary held firm. Mary's folks were unhappy at the service, and her dad was short and critical with Jerry. Yet the wedding went forward. Jack, Bill, Mary, Patty and I were all in the wedding party. Everyone in the college Flock circle confirmed this marriage despite the parents' objections.

It did not go well with Jack and Susan, however. He found himself in conflict with her; they were not "flowing" together. They tried to feel love, but it was not forthcoming. Finally Jack decided to speak to a charismatic leader at a conference in Detroit. After much discussion with Susan, he decided to break the relationship. As a result of some of these experiences, it was decided to no longer have prayer groups operating separately from congregational authority.

THE GREAT MIRACLE

Life continued as always until the night of the "great miracle." We gathered for an especially powerful evening of worship. In the past when I would question the Flock Church, Jack would often say, "You know it is of God. Where else is there an expression of worship to compare with it?" That evening was certainly a demonstration of Jack's words.

During the period of prophecy, a mother brought her child for healing. Apparently, her legs were paralyzed. A group gathered in a circle to lay hands on her and pray. Finally they took the girl by the hand and began to encourage her to walk. She took a feeble step with adult support. People began to praise God in song. She took another step. They praised more loudly. She took two shaky, slow steps by herself, and they began to praise with all their might. Then the little girl walked, and finally ran, to her mother. Everyone was ecstatic. Joy and exaltation were thicker than can be imagined. A new day had dawned.

This was the opportunity I had longed for – a possible *bona fide* miracle. I hoped to find the mother after the service to obtain the medical records.

It took a while to break through the throng of people congratulating her. When I did, I asked a question no one had thought to ask. "What was wrong with your child?" Her answer was, "Oh, nothing I can pin down. She came home from school yesterday and plopped on the floor saying, 'Mommy, I cannot walk.' I took her to the doctor, and he said there was nothing wrong with her. He said she was just going through a psychological stage and when she wants to walk, she will.'"

What a let down! I too was praising and believing that at last this might be a Scriptural-type miracle. Now it seemed clear; it was only the crowd encouragement which gave the girl the motivation to walk.

While traveling home with my friends, I shared my disappointment. They discounted it by saying, "A healing is a healing. If it was only psychological, it was a wonderful healing of the girl's emotions." They missed the point of my concern. An emotional healing carried no apologetic, evidential value.

Over the next week on campus, I was surprised to hear the spread of the story of a great, supernatural miracle. It was said that an amazing healing of a paralytic had taken place and had been witnessed by hundreds. Invitations to attend Flock Church were given to students. These invitations included the story of that healing.

I was upset by this turn of events. I saw it as deceptive. Therefore, I went to talk with Dr. Ziegler, the Christian existentialist philosopher. He encouraged me not to get bent out of shape, that psychological healing was important, that no one was intentionally deceiving, and that I should just let it pass. Perhaps if we would receive the power of God by faith for small things (colds, aches, and psychological problems) we would later see healing in the areas of tumors and atrophied limbs. "Be patient and seek to develop faith," he counseled.

Seeking to pin down a miracle was very difficult. I would hear of a cancerous tumor which was healed, but when I would check it out – it proved far from certain. Once Jerry claimed he saw a cancer tumor disappear. I questioned how he knew it was cancer. He replied that he assumed the lump on the man's neck was cancer.

"Did it really disappear?" I asked.

"Well, sort of," he replied, "although it did not go away completely. It appeared to me to shrink."

I was having a very hard time finding a real miracle at Flock Church, and I wondered how many miracles in the charismatic movement were the product of the same wishful thinking and enthusiasm I had seen at Flock.

Since that time, I am thrilled to say, I have more than substantiated many *bona fide* miracles. Most of them have been in charismatic circles, though many were also in non-charismatic groups. The first was a Lutheran friend who was healed at the point of death from a severed main artery in his neck. He is today a minister. Many miracles through Kathryn Kuhlman were authentic, and one of her case histories described a student at Wheaton. This was not enough to settle all my faith questions, however. There seemed to be real miracles, though not at Flock Church.

MULTIPLE ERRORS

During the winter several tendencies became an established and pronounced part of Flock's *perspective*. These tendencies were the main factors responsible for our leaving Flock.

Several members of the congregation had been convinced that practical perfection was possible on the basis of the baptism in the Holy Spirit. From this practical perfection would come an amazing number of miraculous manifestations. Yet anger, lust, selfishness, impure thoughts and anxiety were still experienced from time to time. When sin still manifested in their lives, they were greatly discouraged. Perfectionism proved to be a doctrine of discouragement.

Furthermore, many began to see that the miracle stories that had been so enthusiastically spread were very insubstantial. It seemed as if the sense of the miraculous grew more and more dim. This was the age in which theologians were saying "God is dead" or at least hidden. To many at Flock, it seemed as if God were indeed hidden. Unfulfilled expectations led to discouragement, which confirmed this fear. Why would this be? Had we not received the Holy Spirit baptism? Did we not go through water baptism in the name of Jesus with faith in the cutting off of the old person?

The response of the pastor was expressed through his teaching. First, it was emphasized that our private interpretations of Scripture needed to be submitted to the local body. Indeed, the local body was said to be the source for our understanding of Scripture. Apart from the congregation, it was said, we really could not adequately understand the Scriptures. At first this emphasis was very low key. Many understood it to mean that we needed the input of brothers and sisters and leadership to come to fuller understanding in the Spirit. Whenever the question of the authority of the Scriptures came up, Pastor Tabor would assure everyone that his speech was not yet clear in expressing the revelation of the importance of the congregation as a teaching authority. He explained, "Don't worry about it at this time, since it is not yet clear." Yet over the next year this emphasis grew to the point whereby some gave up reading the Scriptures altogether so as to get their teaching only from the congregation.

Under the leadership of Pastor Tabor's teaching as well as prophetic messages from the members, the congregation developed several significant doctrines. First, it was said that the congregation needed to go through a wilderness period before entering the promised land of miracles and perfection. This was the process of dying with Christ (Romans 6). The preaching, week after week, emphasized only Romans 6 and the Israel wilderness experience. Dying with Christ and going through the wilderness could take a long time. We were not yet dead and resurrected. The second development was a subtle but steady growth in the doctrine which stated that the intellect was a primary barrier to receive spiritual things. The "crucifixion of the intellect" doctrine became more prominent toward the end of 1969.

Shortly before I left the congregation, the editor of the campus magazine and I had a conversation. She had heard that I planned to attend Trinity Evangelical Divinity School for a Philosophy of Religion degree. She asked, "Isn't that against your faith?"

"I hope not," I said.

Indeed, if the mind does not weigh truth and test for error, how shall we avoid falling into falsehood? We must "test the spirits."

This *anti-intellect doctrine* slowly evolved into a reaction against what was called "dead Evangelical orthodoxy" which was said to be gangrene to spiritual life, a destructive cancer. Some students influenced by a neo-orthodox view of Scripture applauded these teachings. They held that the Scripture is not the Word, but it only becomes the Word when used by the Spirit in the context of the congregation. This is the essence of the neo-orthodox view. Due to the prominence of this view, I found myself attending less often.

The last doctrine held that we were *awaiting the formation of Christ in us.* We were in the pangs of birth, waiting to deliver. The book of First John references Jesus' coming in the flesh, which was interpreted to mean Jesus formed in the body. Several questioned this view and noted that these passages referred to the heresies that claimed Jesus really didn't become human flesh. The historic context of First John is a reply to those who denied the *real incarnation* (into flesh) of the LORD. The response by Pastor Tabor was that the intellect was blocking spiritual truth, and we needed to receive spiritual truth spiritually.

He also denied that in teaching this spiritual application that he was saying anything contrary to the historic incarnation. But what was considered important was the *spiritual meaning* of the passage as *the Spirit* was *applying it in our present situation.* The over-concern with historic events was said to be a false pre-occupation of dead orthodoxy.

Of crucial significance was Flock's relationship to the rest of the Body during these times. The doctrines taught by Pastor Tabor were strongly affirmed by the prophetic flow during the service and by the members outside of the service – through amazing dreams, visions, and prophecies. Yet other leaders in the Body questioned the direction Pastor Tabor was taking, especially in regard to the First John interpretations and the "manifest sons of God" doctrine.

This latter doctrine emphasized the second coming or return of Jesus as having reference to His coming in the church, or the church being perfected in Him. At Flock, both the *incarnation* (His coming in the flesh) and the second coming were being spoken of more and more in terms of Jesus being formed in us: the congregational body being brought to perfection – or the resurrection life of Jesus in us. However, it was constantly emphasized that we were in the crucifixion stage, the wilderness stage, or the dying stage. Other leaders who had related to Flock (Ern Baxter, Rev. James Beall) began to get wind of this doctrine. They sought to impress upon Pastor Tabor that Flock's teaching was in error, especially in regard to their interpretation related to Jesus' coming in the flesh.

Pastor Tabor's response was withdrawal. He proceeded to subtly tell the Flock members that the Flock leadership was being misunderstood. With great delicacy he shared that Flock Church *was hearing from God in a unique way* that only could be truly understood by the involved members. For a time, until God revealed the same doctrine to others, Flock would need to go through a period of separation, or at least distance from other leaders and congregations. By this separation, God would be able to do His unique work without the confusion and hindrance that would come from other leadership input.

Flock now had established a pattern of inwardness and congregational authority which dominated the lives of its members. For many, their only understanding of Scripture came from the congregation, and there was no input from other leaders. Patty (my future wife) and I could not tolerate any longer the subjectivity of Flock. If our mind did not test doctrine by an objective reading of Scripture, anything could be possible. Hence, after June 1969, we left Flock for good, though we maintained close contact with several Flock members for the next few years.

GRADUAL CHANGE

It might be asked, "How could students from Evangelical homes be so easily drawn into the new doctrines of Flock?" It should be understood that the process of indoctrination was gradual. Pastor Tabor would subtly speak of some aspects of a new doctrine. Usually a significant minority reacted negatively. His response to this negative feedback was to pull away, variously saying, "I didn't mean it that way." "The Spirit is not yet clear enough." "We must not prejudge until there is greater clarity." "Let's put this on the back burner because I am not yet sure if I spoke correctly." These responses would satisfy the critics.

Amazingly, however, prophetic words and vivid dreams would confirm the message over the weeks to follow. Later the pastor would again teach the doctrine with new aspects. This time fewer would object. People began to see how it could be so; thus they got used to the idea. Again there would be a partial pullback. After several times of putting forth a teaching and pulling back, along with many months of apparent prophetic confirmation, eventually almost everyone accepted the doctrine. Those who could not left the congregation.

Because of the closeness of the community which developed, there was a great social pressure to see it Pastor Tabor's way. He was not a strong, domineering leader; yet the pressure was great. If a person did not accept the doctrine, he would lose his friends and the affirming sense of closeness in community. Because doctrine slowly evolved with a pulsation of putting forth and withdrawing, people became desensitized to the most radical points of view. They got used to the ideas. It was like the proverbial frog: if dropped in boiling water, he would jump out immediately. Yet when put into a pot which was slowly brought to a boil, the frog would become accustomed to the gradual increase in temperature and would do nothing.

Another important dimension was the view of, and attitude toward, Evangelicalism and fundamentalism. Both were characterized as dead, legalistic, and intellectualistic at best – a cancer or gangrene at worst. Some students were bitter over legalistic backgrounds and quite negative toward Wheaton, their parents, and their home congregation. These students became influential in the direction of the congregation through the prophetic flow. They would share their prophetic sense with Pastor Tabor, who referred to it as confirmation of his teaching. Pastor Tabor was influenced in his view of Wheaton and Evangelicalism by the views that came from the students. Dreams were also given prominent exposure through mutual sharing, whether privately or in the services. Prophecy also confirmed previously formed views of Evangelicals. Evangelical circles which were anti-charismatic were pointed out, so as to confirm the judgment.

ERRORS PRODUCED BAD FRUIT

How did this affect people personally? My roommate, Jack, began to doubt the value of his studies. However, there was still a mixture of opinion, even in his own mind. At times he still hoped for reconciliation between the values of education at Wheaton and the spiritual-prophetic dimensions of Flock. Perhaps Flock was really only speaking of an overly intellectualistic approach. Perhaps there was a balanced spiritual approach to study. However, at other times the whole Christian liberal arts endeavor was questioned. It was a time of turmoil for Jack, but he could not leave Flock because the spiritual experience was so dramatically real for him. His experience was paralleled by many others, some of whom came from the ranks of the brighter students at Wheaton.

Part of the attraction to Flock was a new spiritual security in which one had a rationale for not having to deal with the hard questions and challenges of the faith brought by the study of philosophy, psychology, and literature. If these subjects made us uncomfortable and challenged an easy faith, then Flocker's felt perhaps they were suspect. Some who were in the midst of faith reevaluation due to exposure through their studies were feeling adrift indeed. The *innovative* perspective of Flock gave them a *new* sense of the reality of the supernatural.

Some began to bifurcate certain subjects as valid and others as invalid. Many became sociology majors because it was practical. Others saw the natural sciences as valid. Philosophy, theology, literature, anthropology and psychology became forbidden territory. Of course, this *dichotomy* is totally invalid since all sciences raise significant philosophical issues. Conflicting philosophies of science certainly prove this.

One student who left Flock finally rejected the whole Flock mentality. He said to his friend Jeff, "Why don't you refuse your diploma if you really believe in crucifying the intellect?" Jeff accepted the diploma for its pragmatic value in the job market, but said that otherwise he would be glad to burn it. Other students dropped out of school and went to work. For a time this was the case with Jerry and Mary. Eventually Jerry enrolled in another school for a sociology degree for practical purposes. Bill and his girlfriend (eventually wife) Janice took a different approach – to slide by and get the degree while doing as little work as possible. He tried to get C's and eventually to get the degree for practical job purposes. This approach led to his flunking out of school the following year. This brilliant philosophy student who was burdened to become a missionary to France now no longer desired either to go to France or to finish his studies. These patterns were often repeated by others.

SEARCH THE SCRIPTURES

I was a weekly visitor to Wheaton in the 1969-1970 school year because Patty was still a student there. I would stay in one of the men's houses which included several Flock members. I noticed that many were identifying emotionally with aspects of the "hip" culture, the new-left, and the whole "rock" scene. Bill began to do pop art. It reflected a deep cynicism for modern American life. Others began to identify with the last, most pessimistic messages of the Beatles. The only real hope in their view was Flock. Yet that period at Flock brought little significant change. The doctrines of Flock Church became more and more solidified. We were amazed to learn that Flock was still going through the wilderness and waiting for the resurrection.

A conversation with Jack that fall was most alarming, but it paralleled the convictions of many Flock members. When I argued with Jack over Scriptural teaching and issues, the argument usually came to a disagreement of method between Jack's subjective approach to Scripture and my objective approach. Finally Jack said, "Dan, I do not believe that we can understand the Bible unless it comes through the teaching of the congregation. Only the teaching of the congregation is important to me." My response was, "Jack, I believe that the congregation is very important. However, the Scripture must be the source for evaluating the congregation. Sometimes a congregation goes into error and it becomes our responsibility to leave the congregation." I explained how when Martin Luther started the Reformation, he was summoned to appear before the Emperor to defend himself. His interrogator asked him, "Martin, how is it that you presume to stand against the judgment of Popes and councils and even the whole tradition of church interpretation?" Luther replied, "Whether there be Popes, they have erred and sinned, and councils have gone astray. If anyone can convince me from the Scriptures that I am in error, I shall wholly repent. However, if not, I must say that my mind is captive to the Word of God. Here I stand, I can do no other." I concluded by asking Jack, "What if Flock Church goes into gross error? What will you do? Will you not have to choose God and the Word over and above a particular congregation?" Jack answered, "I cannot separate my commitment to God from my commitment to Flock. They are one and the same. If Flock goes down the tubes, I go with it."

At this point I realized that the battle was lost. There was no further argument. Similar conversations were held with Jerry and Mary with the same frustrating results. There was no way to break through. There was no point of common ground from which to argue them out of their previously drawn conclusions. Some of Flock's members had given up the ability of independent evaluation.

RESCUED FROM FURTHER DETERIORATION AT FLOCK

My first year at Trinity was still a period of doubt and searching; however, little by little, God began to reveal Himself to me. My studies began to confirm the Scriptures. By the end of 1970, God had supernaturally spoken to my heart via the Word, dreams, and study. I now was clearly becoming established in the faith. At Trinity I saw great piety merged with scholarship in such wonderful men as Dr. R. Longenecker, Dr. K. Kantzer, Dr. E. Harrison, and Dr. David Wells. It was a marvelously liberating experience. Patty and I found ourselves growing more and more apart from Flock friends, some of whom had been our closest friends. We attended an Evangelical Lutheran congregation under a dear, saintly pastor named Rev. Theodore Laesch. His example and teaching provided a healing experience. The Lutheran service of communion was a beautiful means to draw us close to God. We even considered the Lutheran pastorate. Continued contact with Dr. Evan Welsh was still greatly restorative. Later I accepted my first pastorate in Chicago at the First Hebrew Christian Church. Chaplain Welsh had been interim pastor and recommended me to the elders. Eventually I was ordained in the United Presbyterian Church.

During this period, Dr. Welsh also became alarmed at the trends of Flock. He who had been so open and accepting was now definitely opposed. The year 1971 saw Flock members adopt the posture of refusing to visit other congregations. "They are dead places of idolatry," they said. Students also became severely divided from parents. Indeed, it was the Flock perspective that it might be necessary for some to cut off relationships with parents.

At this time we also began to perceive a strange looseness among some Flock members. Speech included swearing and other loose, demeaning language. At Trinity I met a new friend named Russ Savage. Russ, a tall and lanky Canadian, was a philosophical thinker in my same Trinity program. He, Patty and I were invited to a party at Jerry and Mary's apartment. The lights were dim, the rock music blared, and the Flock members at the party danced with sensual abandon. Some retired to other rooms to share passionate embracing and kissing. We saw no nudity, nor any blatant sinful activities. Yet the atmosphere was sensually charged. After the party, Russ remarked, "Listen, that group is weird. I have been involved with secular groups at the university. I have been to their parties. I have even seen them degenerate into sin. That was just plain old-fashioned secular sin. This party had a strange dimension. It was something on another level. These people were expressing deep and negative reactions to their background as part of their sin. There was an attitude and atmosphere that is thoroughly unhealthy beyond anything I have experienced."

I agreed with Russ. How perceptive were his words! The previous summer I had spoken with the elder, Larry Carroll, who had first introduced me to the baptism in the Spirit. When I explained the treatment of Scripture at Flock, he predicted, "The next step is immorality." Indeed, the next few years at Flock were momentous as elements of destruction came to full manifestation.

Contacts with Flock members during the next two years were less frequent. However, there was enough contact to produce a significant amount of insight. As the year 1971 progressed, Flock members became more intensely permeated by the concept of the wilderness state of their existence. They accepted themselves as spiritually dead and in need of resurrection. Their hope was in a supernatural renewal that would produce immediate perfection. The only spiritual reality was the prophetic dimension at Flock, and the members were more and more withdrawn into their own community. The leadership at Flock emphasized the importance of not visiting other communities, along with not sharing the revelation coming forth with people outside the community. "They wouldn't understand."

Patty and I were exceptions to this rule. First, we were perceived as more open and still searching. Second, we had been close friends with the members. The changes during 1971 were not totally radical. Members became more tightly knit. They partied together, worked together, and waited together.

Bill and Janice lived in a small bungalow and drifted into a more and more nihilistic concept of life while maintaining their Flock hope. He began to develop an interest in auto mechanics which would eventually provide his living. Jack worked at various jobs not requiring specific training. He gained an interest in large motorcycles and wore granny glasses. This was an incredible change in Jack's personality. Jerry began to develop an interest in computers. It was a financially solid field, and this eventually became his career choice. The sociology professor continued to teach her classes, although they became more and more lacking in content. The philosophy teacher, Dr. Ziegler, transferred to a secular college, but he no longer sought to find truth in philosophy.

Many people experienced great conflicts in their marriages. In addition, many found it necessary to cut off relationships with old friends and relatives, especially parents. Parents became alarmed, but they found no way to correct the errors they saw or to regain the trust of their children. Slowly the character of our friends also began to change. There was more and more willingness to use loose language and to indulge in worldly entertainment. Not only seedy rock music, but R and X-rated motion pictures were considered acceptable. "It is good to know the real world," some would say. It was considered important to break out of fundamentalist structures. The goals of many became more focused upon immediate pleasures. For some, this was reflected in materialistic desires, for others in the adoption of the appearance and attitudes of the sixties counterculture. Covert sex among singles, and possibly even others, began at this time, but it was not condoned behavior.

Slowly, the atmosphere of Flock began to change as well. This evolution followed their theology. "If we are spiritually dead, in the process of dying or going through the wilderness, how can we be singing worship songs and taking the LORD's supper? Does baptism even work in our present situation?" These questions led to a gradual cessation of these practices. The services became primarily an exercise in hearing revelation and in absorbing the sermons of Pastor Tabor. During this period the congregation began to lose members. Some saw no point to it at all. Flock had been their last hope; as a result they became secular. Others went back to Evangelical expressions of faith. Still others said they still believed in Flock, but did not really need to attend at this point. The leaders of Flock saw this as a necessary stage toward the goal of perfection. "We are being pruned and getting to the real core of our membership," Pastor Tabor said. "When the resurrection comes, all those who have been connected to us will return." This was all part of the wilderness experience. The Flock members subjectively spiritualized and allegorized all things.

Our limited experiences with Flock members were extremely valuable for obtaining information. Jerry and Mary related much to us, and Jack filled in many of the gaps. We learned that various couples were separating, and some were even seeking divorce. This included our friends Janice and Bill. What a tragedy! The future missionary to France, the brilliant student, and his Pentecostal wife now with seemingly ruined lives. We did not know the half of it.

The next few visits with Jerry and Mary provided all the necessary details. As we sat together, we probed Jerry and Mary for updated information on Flock Church. Our friends had become part of the inner core. Finally the bombshell was dropped. Mary had given herself to extramarital affairs. Jerry had committed adultery as well. However, we were told not to be alarmed because it was all part of the process leading to the resurrection and perfection of the Church. Many of the young couples had swapped mates and had extramarital affairs. Bill had moved in with a forty-plus woman.

How was all of this justified? Mary explained their reasoning. "If we really are in a spiritually dead state or dying process waiting for the resurrection, then to continue to seek to follow a rigid morality would only be hypocrisy. To give in to the desires within us would be a step of honesty. When Pastor Tabor first heard about various members sleeping together, he expressed worry that it could destroy Flock. Yet, he realized it might be a necessary stage in the process toward the resurrection. Indeed, there was revelation to confirm that this was a necessary stage. The physical nature is not all that important; therefore, to indulge it does not matter. What is important is not physical adultery, but spiritual adultery or idolatry. Evangelicals are un-resurrected and are making a pretense of morality though they are obviously imperfect. This is spiritual adultery; a terrible sin. Since they are dead, but yet are worshipping in their services, they must be serving and worshipping a false god. We should not be preoccupied with sex, but at this stage, if we must indulge, it is better to do so than to live in the tension which comes from resisting. I have had two dreams to confirm this. When I explained them to Pastor Tabor, he confirmed them. They speak to the situation of Flock."

Mary continued and explained her dream. "In one I was sitting on a river bank beneath a dam full of water. Then the dam burst. I was full of fear and sought to escape from the rush of the water, but I could not. After the flood, I found myself in a place of calm and peace farther downstream where the waters no longer raged. I was swept along, but unharmed. The waters represented stored up passions and desires. They had to be released. However, releasing them would not ultimately harm me. In the other dream, a one-horned beast charged me and pushed its horn into my chest. Rather than dying, although it hurt, I felt purified or cleansed. When it was plunged in, I was cleansed."

Mary had sex with a secular man who was not part of Flock. She described it as enjoyable because he was a "neat guy" but also painful in a way. Jerry had an experience of a similar kind. Now that they had done this, they claimed they were freer and not hung up. They could attend nude bars and other worldly places without being uptight. Others were having similar experiences. It was all part of waiting for the resurrection.

I reflected during this conversation on how similar this teaching was to the heretics in the early centuries who were called *libertarian gnostics*. They had rigidly divided the spiritual and the physical. The latter was of no consequence. Therefore, the indulgence of the flesh proved its insignificance and liberated the spirit. As Ecclesiastes says, "There is nothing new under the sun." I expressed my disagreement, but I knew if I opposed them too strongly, they would have left our company for good. Mary was amazingly "hung up" about the mistakes and harm her parents had caused. This surfaced constantly in conversation.

The last extensive visit we had with Mary and Jerry shed further light on the situation of Flock. The teaching had taken on a decidedly eastern twist. They were seeking the God beyond God who could not be spoken of but was only to be experienced beyond concepts and words. However, words were said to be vehicles to break down all the illusions of false religion so they could experience the true God. Historical knowledge was unimportant. The resurrection of Jesus was not denied, but the question of its historical reality was unimportant since its only significant meaning was the spiritual resurrection to come. "It makes no difference whether it happened in the physical," they said. "Jesus' coming in the flesh is His being formed in us." I was able to probe the question with such understanding that Mary was amazed. This proved to them that I was really part of the fold. However, I explained to them that I was a student of eastern religious philosophy, and this was why I understood. In fact, their view was not a new revelation at all. When I told them this, it strained our visit. It was the last really *significant* contact with them, during which we also learned that one of the sources of revelation at Flock was the son of a Buddhist priest who had married one of the Wheaton students!

Later, at a Wheaton football game, we met Janice. We asked her if she still attended Flock. She said that she did not, but she still felt a part of it. She explained that she was living a secular life and enjoying her *freedom.* "I am a healthy, red-blooded female animal, you know."

Then one morning the phone rang. "Hello, Dan? This is Jack. How are you?"

"Fine, and you?"

"Not too good; I'm in the hospital. Would you like to visit with me?"

Jack was a patient in a renowned psychiatric hospital in the area. He had crashed. The experience with Jack which followed this phone call gave me many missing details about Flock. Through him I learned much concerning the sources and implications of cultic bondage. As we sat in Jack's hospital room, he told me some of the sad details that led to his hospitalization. Some were into astrology as a means of understanding reality. This was prevalent among younger rather than older members. He also described a more rampant sexual looseness among couples than we had even imagined. There were parties that ended in orgies. Drugs were also part of the experience among some. He stated that some of the parties even took on a "Charles Manson type atmosphere." There was such suspicion that I thought it would end in violence.

Drugs, women, and conceptual confusion produced an identity crisis in Jack. The night Jack "freaked out," he thought that he was John the Baptist. He was taken to the hospital, paranoid to the extreme. Pastor Tabor signed him in.[3] When the door locked behind him in the ward, he went berserk and had to be strapped down. He was having delusions and had also experienced some fearful drug flashbacks. Since Pastor Tabor had previously referred to Jack as Flock's John the Baptist, a forerunner of what the congregation would eventually come to, the direction of Jack's delusion was understandable. Thankfully Jack was blessed with a fine psychiatrist, a man open to the spiritual dimensions of psychiatric problems. After therapy and treatment, Jack was eventually able to be released for visits with us and finally came to stay as a boarder. When Jack came to live with us he was full of fear, bitterness, anxiety, mistrust, irrational thought, and double-mindedness. He wondered why had he been allowed to be so deceived? At times he slipped back into the Flock mentality. Twice he ran away – once even running back to Flock. The other time he went to New York state where a former Flock member who had a similar experience had found help in a Christian community. For a time he lived with his very worried mother and stepfather. Yet he found help and promise in being with us. His psychiatrist and I could provide greater counsel and understanding. So finally Jack returned to stay with Patty and me. This lasted until his marriage.

After walking off many jobs within the first few days because of waves of uncontrollable fear, Jack stuck with a job as a cab driver. With much counsel, conversation, and prayer – including the dimensions of deliverance from occult bondage – Jack came to a real state of psychological health. The medication was discontinued. He became his old self with the broad smile, and the love of life returned. He was healed.

---

[3]   Seeing Jack "freak out" really disturbed Jerry and Mary. Jerry was on the verge of breaking from Flock. However, even though he was in a state of real anxiety, he was unable to break away. Furthermore, his wife was holding firm.

Chapter 2

Why Did It Happen?

We are entering a phase of history in which social upheaval is prevalent. If at any time in history stable and mature leadership was needed in the Body, today is that day. This brings us to our first reason for the tragedies of Flock Church – inadequate leadership. All the factors to be discussed are crucial danger signs. They should awaken reservations before deciding to join or continue with any particular congregation, but the first factor is especially vital.

Inadequacy of Leadership According to Scriptural Criteria

Pastor Tabor was not the usual image of a cultic leader. He was not domineering, and he did not command the worship or adoration of his followers. He indeed was stubborn once he had formed a conviction. The experiences at Flock convinced me that a strong cultic figure is not necessary for the development of a devastatingly destructive community. *Inadequacy of leadership, however, seems always to be a crucial factor.*

Pastor Tabor was a liberal Protestant with *little solid Scriptural background*. When he and his congregation switched from the liberal-humanistic mode to evangelical-charismatic, Pastor Tabor had little background or qualification to lead the congregation in its new mode of belief. There was very *limited* background for *spiritual discernment*. In truth, Pastor Tabor was a new believer, and new believers are not quickly to be raised to leadership or they can be puffed up with pride (1 Timothy 3:6).

It was pride that led to Pastor Tabor's refusal to hear and be corrected by other leaders. Hence, he cut off relations with the rest of the Body. As a new believer, he was ill-prepared to deal with the spiritual phenomena at Flock. Soon liberal ideas concerning Scriptural inspiration and authority from his seminary studies were drawn upon when they fit the need to break from Scripture to support ecstatic prophecies and dreams.

Pastor Tabor's own spiritual stability was of real concern. He often exhibited depression, confusion, mood swings, pride, and hurt. There was certainly a measure of compassion and some desire for truth, yet pride superseded it. Because Pastor Tabor had never been a leader under proper spiritual authority, he did not know how to lead in a proper spiritual manner. The possibility of a variety of motives and inspirations in prophecy escaped his perception. The intricacies of human depravity and its manifestations in individuals and groups were certainly not part of his spiritual training or experience.

Other people in leadership at Flock were as weak in experience as Pastor Tabor, with one exception. This was an elder with an Evangelical seminary background, but he was swept along with the congregation. Although there were a few professors of the Christian college who went along with the teaching of Flock, they were not in direct leadership. They were either weak in personal stability or had exhibited a history of hurt and disappointment. Some who did not exhibit a psychological instability were *spiritually and theologically weak* even though they were well educated in their respective academic disciplines.

Leadership which is weak in spiritual experience, Scriptural theology, and personal stability is dangerous leadership. I have come to the conclusion that a stable, satisfying family life is a literal prerequisite for governmental leadership in the Body. An elder leader must first be a man proven in spiritual leadership in the home, then in responsibility under other mature leaders. Only then should he be raised to leadership in his own right (I Timothy 3).

One should also note the phenomenon of paranoia in many groups that go astray. This begins with the milder claim of "they would not be able to understand," but degenerates to the level of "they are out to get us." This begins among the leadership and filters down to the people. This must be distinguished from legitimate guardedness toward the forces of evil. The fear of others from differing communities arises from deep insecurity. A person with such fear cannot engage those who disagree in constructive dialogue. This paranoia was certainly in the Flock leadership and led to their isolationism. We who know the LORD or who are on the cutting edge of a new work of the Spirit need never to fear other basically moral believers. We must not cut ourselves off. Separatism is heresy.

Why did people trust themselves to Flock's weak leadership? It was because the miraculous was supposedly happening. This was a weak criterion for choosing leadership; however, once the choice had been made, the motivation of maintaining the social context of meaningful relationships with others at Flock became very strong.

BITTERNESS AND PROPHETIC DIRECTION

No one who stayed committed to Flock was willing to raise the difficult question of the sources of inspiration. According to Scripture, one may be inspired by self (or the flesh), evil spirits, or the Holy Spirit. Therefore, Scripture enjoins us to test the spirits, to prove that which is good (Deuteronomy 13 and 18; 1 John 4:1). We have found that people are open to deception when their hearts are not full of love, forgiveness and humility.

Many of the students of Flock were in a state of bitterness, pride, and unhealed hurt. They were bitter at the legalistic restrictions of fundamentalist backgrounds, bitter toward their parents, and bitter toward the college's authority and rules. The desire for something new, to break from the past, was great among some. Many were as the proverbial first psychology student who thought he had discovered what was wrong with his parents. Among some, this ushered in an attitude of rebellion to all authority including the college, parents, and the Evangelical leaders.

Scripture also says that rebellion and bitterness lead to false prophecy. These attitudes open the door to evil spirits which can also inspire; the attitudes themselves produce a perspective on life and reality which influences prophecy. Hence, Evangelicalism was seen to be "gangrene." Pastor Tabor was readily influenced by the perspective of the students. *The hearts of people are the second most crucial factor leading to cultic error!* Before they fell into error, their hearts were impure.

This leads us to examine the integral relationship between submitting to true authority and false authority. This relationship exhibits a pattern we have seen over and over again since our experience in Flock, a pattern not usually recognized by writers in these areas.

There are several authority spheres taught in Scripture. They include the authority of the state (government), the family, and the Body. The basic boundaries between authority spheres, and the limits and extents of authority within each, are Scripturally derived. We are enjoined to give obedience to the law of the land and its magistrates, but never contrary to Scripture (Acts 5:29; Romans 13). We are enjoined to submit to congregational leadership, but never contrary to the Apostolic foundations of teaching or to the detriment of one's conscience and thinking ability (Hebrews 13:17). Leaders are exhorted to correct, rebuke, discipline, and to set the pattern of organization and responsibility in the congregation.

We must never let cultic authority cause us to shrink from affirming the fact that the Scripture sets forth the importance of real authority vested in human beings by God, and that authority is to be respected. Any congregation that is not in immorality, exercises discipline, and preaches the truth is of God. To oppose the congregation negatively is to oppose the Spirit of God and to fall into dangerous oppression. Yet in our age, rebellion to authority of all kinds has been rampant. Lawlessness affects both the congregation and society. So it was in the college among Evangelical students. The spirit of the 1960's rebellion had affected even us! Yet one of the strange but true paradoxes is that when there is rebellion against proper, balanced authority within Scriptural limits and extents, the person becomes a target for cultic authority and demonic control. Why is this the case? It is because proper authority, though requiring respect and teachability, never violates the mind or conscience of the individual. Even the Holy Spirit only prompts us and seeks to woo us to willingly obey His promptings. Evil spirits, however, are perfectly willing to place us into a bondage of the will. We need to understand that pride and the severe bitterness of the heart which leads to rebellion opens one up to demonic influence in the same way that direct occult involvement does! This is why the person who rebels against balanced authority will submit to a totally controlling, cultic authority which seeks the suppression of thinking and conscience.

While all leadership is imperfect in some regards, not being willing to submit to imperfect leadership due to pride causes some to look for perfect leadership. Only a pretender can appear to be perfect, and thus delude the proud. For this reason, Reverend Moon is called the "perfect master" by his mesmerized followers. We have seen these patterns over and over again. Only warfare, prayer, and deliverance can free the ones submitted to occult bondage.

How did this pattern fit Flock? Some Flock members were in rebellion against the family, the college, the state, and the Body. They had anger and bitterness toward what was perceived (sometimes incorrectly and sometimes correctly) as an over-strict, narrow upbringing. The congregations of the students' backgrounds were also negatively evaluated because of the spirit of cynicism pervasive in the 1960's. Whenever we do not appreciate our roots and forgive mistakes and sins, a negative spirit of bitterness takes root in our hearts. This bitter root was manifested directly against the college faculty and *especially* the administration. The administration, by setting and enforcing college rules, became the surrogate parents in the students' minds. This explains the severe and almost slanderous criticism of the school and Evangelicalism (a gangrene or a cancer eating away true spiritual life). If a teacher was a boring lecturer, he was not described as uninteresting – but as personally dead spiritually or part of the gangrene of death at the school. Spiritual pride took on an air of great superiority.

As the book of Hebrews warns, the root of bitterness can corrupt many. Therefore students without negative reactions took upon themselves such reactions through the influence of their fellows. If new studies led to some uncertainty, it was because Christian liberal arts was wrong. Why did they not instead consider that they needed to grow and learn more? The spiritual pride of Flock leaders played into the bitter criticisms directed at Evangelicals. Even saintly Chaplain Welsh, who was beloved by all, was looked at in a negative light for he was not yet into the "reality" *we* had experienced!

People in bitterness, rebellion, and pride who open up to the supernatural for revelation speak from the inspiration of their own flesh or evil spirits. There can indeed be a supernatural dimension beyond coincidence, but this does not prove doctrine. To be under the influence of evil spirits and to have power from them *is* witchcraft. This is why rebellion is akin to witchcraft; they are intertwined. Hence, the Flock members who rebelled against proper authority now came under the dominating authority of this particular congregation. It taught them not to read books, not to think, not to hear other religious teachers, not to judge and read Scripture for themselves, and not to further one's education. Indeed, it taught them to get all their understanding from Flock Church. Yet Evangelicals were said to be narrow! Humility and love protect us from delusion. Bitterness and rebellion invariably lead to delusion on some level. Those who intensely rebel *against proper authority* are targets for the Jim Joneses and the more subtle cults with a more decentralized but powerful social-demonic control of members.

Therefore, the second major cause of Flock's destructive direction was that prophetic direction arose from rebellious, bitter, or proud hearts which were thereby subject to the influence of evil spirits. This spiritual pride was so intense that it claimed that only we were hearing the Spirit. Yet "testing the spirits" (1 John 4) was ignored.

SCRIPTURE AS AN OBJECTIVE REVELATION

The third major or significant cause of the deception at Flock was the *loss of Scripture as an objective revelation*. Scripture is emphatic about the importance of testing future revelation by what has been previously and foundationally established. Deuteronomy 13 emphasized that Israel was not to follow any prophet, even if there were supernatural signs and predictions, if teaching concerning God and His relationship to Israel contradicted established revelation in the Torah. Many passages can be appealed to for this principle:

1) In 2 Timothy 3:16-17 Paul teaches that the Bible is inspired by God and is the basis for doctrine, correction and instruction in righteousness.
2) Galatians warns of anyone who teaches another gospel other than that laid down by Apostolic teaching (Galatians 1:7-8). Scripture is Apostolic teaching in writing.
3) Apostolic instruction is to be believed and obeyed (2 Thessalonians 3:14-15; 1 Timothy 6:3-5).

We are especially warned to test the spirits to see if they come from God (1 John 4:1). It is significant that the first doctrine undercut at Flock *was this very one* of how to test the spirits. The specific doctrine used here as a test is the incarnation, that Jesus (God the Son) came in the flesh. This is not the only test, nor an exhaustive test. This test was given in response to gnostic teaching that claimed that Jesus only appeared to be human flesh, but was not really such. Flock began to question the importance of the historic incarnation and then to interpret this verse to mean Jesus' coming to be formed spiritually in us. This opened the door to full subjectivism in doctrine, since their interpretation of this verse was *the opposite* of the historical contextual meaning. Paul in 1 Thessalonians 5:19-21 gives balanced instruction in regard to prophetic gifts: "*Do not quench the Spirit. Do not despise prophecies. Test all things; hold fast what is good.*"

All of this assumed that Scripture provides us with objective revelation for testing all doctrine. Scripture is the plumb line for evaluating further revelation in the Spirit. Scripture must not be subject to reinterpretation according to prophecy and visions, or *the objective ground for testing will be lost.* Paul in Colossians 2:8 warns against those who take their stand on the basis of dreams and visions and are *puffed up* with idle notions.

How does Scripture become the basis for testing new revelation? It does so through the mind. Passage after passage exhorts us to *think!* The mind is the organ of ability for comparing propositions and discovering contradiction or incoherence. The mind must do its work humbly, without intellectual pride. The mind must recognize the importance of intuitive perception in the realm of Spirit to spirit. Indeed, the mind must submit to Scripture to be renewed toward righteous thinking (Romans 12:2). Yet when all is said and done, the mind must apply the laws of logic to test for contradiction.

Watchman Nee brilliantly described the place of the mind in his second volume of *The Spiritual Man.* Although man's inner spirit is the center of receiving intuitive revelation, it is the mind that searches out revelation and expresses it in propositions (meaningful statements). It is the mind which then compares these statements to revelation in Scripture in regard to doctrine and practice. The spiritual mind is indispensable for avoiding error. The laws of logic are part of the equipment of the mind. Yet at Flock Church the mind was held in suspicion; thinking and logic were in disrepute. Rather than putting to death evil and selfish thinking as part of the old nature, Flock taught the putting to death of the mind itself. While the spirit senses and intuits, the mind comprehends. Having forsaken objective revelation and the mind which evaluates, Flock entered a world in which anything was possible. Their minds evaluated their revelations as true because they seemed to hold together without objective reference to Scripture. The mind was still used to evaluate, but it became a darkened mind, unenlightened by the Word.

My experience has taught me that a community can be properly open to supernatural experience as long as the place of the objective Word and testing remains prominently emphasized.

False prophets will eventually show themselves by contradiction to the Word in doctrine or practice. I know of no exception. The office of a prophet is only for the stable mature believer. Even then, we must never forgo testing and prayerful evaluation. Yes the devil is behind false prophecy. If the devil prophesies only truth, he will have no success in his desire to deceive. His method is to capture a group by first giving true prophecy (in accordance with the Word). Later, when the community places its trust in the voice of a person – caught up in the excitement of the supernatural and losing its resolve to test prophecies – the devil will speak deception. Even so, people with a gift of discernment sense that "something is off" in the false prophet before anything false has been said.

A sad feature during this period was the weakness of the Bible faculty of the college. Just previous to this time, the college had experienced a mass exodus of their best professors to a newly expanding seminary. Some Bible courses were taught by men of mediocre qualities. Some were not men of deep faith and experience, nor inspiring as teachers. Today the college has recovered and has an excellent faculty. Yet here is a word for the Christian colleges. The Bible faculty especially must be staffed by people with the following:

1) Great faith, experience and love for the LORD; personal piety, not just intellectual knowledge, is essential
2) An inspiring classroom ability
3) Solid intellectual ability
4) High personal stability of life

In these four areas, the Bible faculty should be the *best* in the school, when compared to other departments. Impressionable minds will otherwise conclude that the Bible is less relevant than other academic subjects – or that the Evangelical faith is dry and not where the life of the Spirit is to be found. Weaknesses in this regard further spurred the drift away from solid Scriptural moorings at Flock.

It is crucial that the charismatic movement gain a deeper commitment to the importance of testing as well as objective, Scriptural scholarship. Allegorical interpretations which play fast and loose with the meaning of texts out of context must be rejected. The Scriptural text can be an illustration or a catalyst for another idea directly taught in the text, but the teacher should never imply that the text itself speaks something other than what is derived from interpretation in its grammatical historical *context*. As has been rightly stated, "A text without context is a pretext."

Additionally, a knowledge of basic Christian history might have been a great antidote to the sense of discovering new revelations. The script of Flock Church had been played out before. The libertarian gnostics of the second and third centuries, the radical montanists of this period, and the radical Charismatics who broke from Scriptural authority and followed Thomas Muntzer during Luther's day are prime examples. For this reason, if for no other, we need to have a more basic knowledge of history in our communities.

In summary, *no believer should ever yield to any group which destroys thinking and the principles of Scripture as an objective revelation and source for testing.*

Preoccupation With Miracles

The fourth major area causing spiritual ruin came from Flock's *preoccupation with miracles and power as opposed to love.* This preoccupation was so great that *miracles of imagination* were spoken of as if they were objectively real. When we examine the miracle accounts of the New Testament, in general we find that love and compassion motivated Jesus to free people from the bondage of sickness and disease. Yes, the signs and wonders confirmed the preaching of the gospel. Yet signs and wonders were not valued for their own sake or for the heady feeling of power. Rather, the power of love motivated the preaching, and *faith and love together in the power of the Spirit produced miracles.* This is a subtle but crucial distinction. A sense of dealing with the supernatural can be very exhilarating. However, this sense can have three sources.

First, the flesh can cause our imagination to run wild. This was the case with the miracles Jerry reported and with the paralyzed little girl. It is true that believers see the hand of God in events that do not prove a direct intervention of God in the natural order. This is legitimate. Yet Flock members claimed stupendous interventions when there were none.

Secondly, the supernatural can be directed by the devil and his hosts. Events certainly occurred which were beyond coincidence. This did not confirm God's *approval.*

Finally, faith and love in the true anointing of God produces miracles. Miracles are not to be sought after for their own sake or power, but are by-products of other central motives. When we seek power for its own sake, we connect to evil spirits. When we seek love, we connect to God.

METHODS INDOCTRINATION

A fifth explanation of Flock's deception relates to the methodology of indoctrination. This was not a planned methodology, but it was just as effective nonetheless. The slow process of indoctrination and the social influence of peers in the community together formed a powerful motive to adopt Flock's radical reinterpretation of Scripture. Doctrinal aberrations were put forth gradually, then withdrawn, and reintroduced repeatedly until the community was no longer shocked by the new way of thinking. Thus the changes seemed more minor than they really were. Each stage was only one part of the whole view. It is parallel to the young person in high school who has heard of the dangers of lung cancer. His peers urge him to try "just one puff" of a cigarette. "One puff can't hurt you," they say. Next he is encouraged to have a whole cigarette. Before long, he is a smoker. So at Flock it was "just take a puff of radical doctrine. It's only a small change; it can't hurt that much. So why not?" Then a whole new doctrine was inhaled. Eventually, a whole new theology was adopted using some Scriptural language, but it was diametrically opposed to Scriptural teaching. We can call this phenomenon gradualism and the influence of strong social pressure from peer groups. Gradualism is the "boiling the frog" phenomenon described earlier. The combination of gradualism and peer pressure is a major influence causing many to succumb to cults. Flock provided the center of meaningful relationships for many, and there was a strong inducement to remain in the fold.

ISOLATIONISM

A sixth important component in Flock's demise was the *decision for isolation*. No one was allowed to speak into the life of the congregation from the outside. It was said, "They wouldn't understand." We never outgrow our need to be teachable, to learn from others, and to be accountable to others. Yet, *in pride* they cut off their relationships with other charismatic and non-charismatic leaders. This is a major mark of cultic direction in a group. An inability to hear from others is the mark of insecurity which seeks to shield itself from any criticism. The claim that others would not be able to understand expanded to the point that only "the initiated" could be admitted to secret revelation. Against this gnostic claim of secret mysteries, the New Testament gospel is a revelation of depth that is proclaimed openly to all. The first two chapters of Colossians and Ephesians were written to counter the argument of those who held to a secret-mystery view of revelation.

SUMMARY

Flock Church both followed and broke the mold of what is usually seen as the path to cultic bondage:

1) There was no strong cultic leader who personally dominated the lives of his followers.
2) There were no blatant brainwashing techniques, such as long hours of lectures, lack of sleep, and "love-bombing" (surrounding the person with love, hugs and words of encouragement in the midst of a long, sleepless regimen).

Yet the method of gradualism and social influence was just as effective in producing conformity. Other dimensions were certainly parallel to the cults. These were:

1) Twisting of Scriptural passages (called Bible-bending by Jim Sire)
2) Social pressures to accept prevailing radical views
3) The denial of key orthodox doctrines

Yet what is so important about Flock is *where it did not* conform to the cults, enhancing the subtlety of its early errors. Today's danger often comes from groups which appear on the surface to be acceptable. However, whenever a group allows bitterness and rebellion to become important motives in congregational direction, the devil can begin to control and direct the life of that congregation and the people in it. Once the devil has control over a group he can supernaturally act through his hosts of hell to use this group for his ends. No strong leader is necessary. Mature, stable leadership is the safeguard against the wiles of the devil. Proper authority on the basis of Scripture is an antidote to error. Sadly we have had personal contact with communities in recent times whose development amazingly parallels Flock.

In summary, we list those marks and danger signs reflected at Flock Church. Use them to aid in your own discernment:

1) Roots of bitterness in a significant segment of people who are giving direction in the congregation, including
   a. Prophecy motivated by pride and rebellion
   b. Rebellion against proper authority in congregational members' lives – rejection of Scripturally ordered groups

2) Spiritual pride – "We are better than others."
3) The rejection of Scripture as an *objective revelation* for testing all teaching and prophecy; e.g., spiritualizing or allegorizing Scripture
4) Disparaging the proper place of the mind and thinking in testing doctrine; e.g., the mind must be crucified; a radical division between mind and spirit
5) Neglect of the lessons of history
6) A desire for miraculous power without the desire for love and service
7) A subtle methodology of slow indoctrination – putting forth and withdrawing radical viewpoints
8) A strong social influence to accept prevailing views
9) Isolation from other leaders and groups
10) Revelation seen as a secret mystery; only the initiated can understand
11) Supernatural phenomena without Scriptural evaluation
12) Untested immature leadership not fitting the standards of 1 Timothy 3

CHAPTER 3

AFTERWARD

After leaving Flock Church, we were turned off to the claims
of the charismatic movement. For a time, my wife and I became
Evangelical rationalists. I believed in God and that He ordered
my existence. Yet guidance in life only came by applying ethical
standards and empirical-rational considerations to circumstances.
I radically held that the Holy Spirit never revealed Himself. If
someone came to the rational conclusion that Jesus was LORD,
the Holy Spirit was involved in this, but imperceptibly. The Holy
Spirit only pointed to Jesus, and this Jesus was the historical Jesus
and the Jesus in heaven, not the present experience of Jesus.

Patty and I attended an Evangelical Lutheran congregation
and found healing in the hymns, the liturgy, and the LORD's
Supper. Yes, God was real, but I was running from the irrational
subjectivism I called "charismania." People on opposite poles
said, "Thus saith the LORD," and I had had enough of that!
As yet I did not understand the intuitive, spiritual side of man's
being – nor the workings of the devil. After two years of graduate
school, two years of seminary and many years in the pastorate, I
have come to some clear, hopefully more balanced conclusions.

I want to share my progression of experiences with you. Perhaps it will be helpful.

The study of Scripture convinced me that the supernatural gifts of the Holy Spirit were not just for one age. Mark 16:17, even if not in the original text, is a clear summary of what the early apostles and disciples believed. The New Testament speaks of spiritual manifestations, miracles, and the gifts of the Spirit as a normal part of life in the Body. The supernatural intervention of God manifested His reality, and confirmed His communication from Genesis to Revelation. The arguments that the gifts of the Spirit were only needed to launch and establish the first century Church were not convincing (see Warfield's *Counterfeit Miracles*). I could not find any texts that supported such an argument, while the evidence I found was quite the opposite. If these gifts were valid then, why not now when unbelief, secularism, and occultism are great indeed? Secondly, I knew of both miracles and manifestations I simply could not discount. There was my Lutheran friend Tom who was supernaturally healed after a car accident. There was Eugene, who was healed of a club foot. Likewise, men of God, who did not identify themselves as Charismatics or Pentecostals, certainly had spiritual gifts. V. Raymond Edman of Wheaton exhibited supernatural words of wisdom and knowledge, and he had many supernatural experiences. Chaplain Evan Welsh exhibited gifts as well. Therefore I concluded that the gifts were real today. They are present among Christians, despite being often unrecognized because they are unnamed. I was, as yet, unconvinced that the gifts of the Spirit were more especially manifest among Charismatics who perhaps were deluded by wishful thinking.

With this viewpoint, I entered the Presbyterian ministry and pastored my first congregation. At this time I also concluded that every believer had the baptism in the Spirit at conversion and that speaking in tongues (the ability I little used) was not a prerequisite to other gifts. I did not yet know of a community that was really practicing the gifts of the Spirit in love and power. Therefore, my ministry was a rational effort type ministry.

Soon after entering the pastorate, two of our members put me in touch with Reba Place Fellowship in Chicago. Fania had a sister in this community, Vera, who invited us for hospitality. Later we attended their services. In those days Reba was a total sharing Christian community. Reba was my first in depth experience with a charismatic community in Scriptural balance. They did not teach tongues as the necessary sign of the "the baptism." However, they manifested prophecy, healing, tongues, interpretation, and other spiritual gifts as part of their corporate and individual lives. There was mature leadership on a firm basis of Scriptural authority, and they were leaders concerned and committed enough to test the spirits. It was marvelous. They had wonderful worship which combined modern and classical elements. There was love, truth, beauty, and goodness. Yes, the charismatic dimension was real and could exist in balance. There was fruit in people's lives, along with the reality of words of wisdom, and the prophetic gifts proved true.

My second great step back to the charismatic world came in experiencing the world of spiritual oppression and the need to free others by deliverance-prayer. I found that people who were unable to gain release in psychiatry or mundane forms of counseling were freed after renunciation and prayer commanding the bonds of the devil to be broken (see K. Koch's many works; M. Bubeck, *The Adversary*). Amazingly, in tough counseling situations, I intuitively received the supernatural discernment of spirits to enable me to help others. At times I knew the problem even before words were even exchanged with a new counselee. There was prayer for healing which showed great results, although perhaps not of a totally provable character for apologetic purposes. Yet probable evidence was there. Since that time, we have seen predictive prophecy fulfilled and healing of a more supernatural character.

Yet, I also knew that my non-charismatic (not anti) professors were men of piety. At times they literally loved their lessons into us, combining a depth of scholarship with faith and love. I could not reject the values of study *nor* the reality of the charismatic dimension. I could not reject the Evangelicals or the Charismatics. Both had given me so much. I needed to think out a new Scriptural approach to the whole subject. Amazingly, great books came to my attention which helped in the search. The mind of man cannot seem to avoid confronting opposing views, and factions will arise. Words both reveal and hide reality. However a humble, searching spirit has the opportunity to transcend limited perspectives to achieve a more adequate viewpoint. One of the discoveries during these years was that of the nineteenth century revivalists.

There was a broad consensus among many giants of the faith from different denominational backgrounds. Charles Finney, D.L. Moody, R.A. Torrey, and Andrew Murray all spoke of the reality of the gifts of the Spirit and the baptism in the Spirit. Murray wrote a book on healing and gained great insight into spiritual gifts. None spoke of tongues as a "sine qua non" sign of the baptism in the Spirit or as a necessary prerequisite to other spiritual gifts. Was it possible that the Pentecostal movement, despite its gain in understanding of spiritual gifts and manifesting the power of God, was the carrier as well of unnecessary division in the Body? Was it also possible that the fundamentalists formed their doctrine in reaction, rather than in humble searching, and thereby created further division?

One thing is clear: powerful supernatural spiritual gifts flowed in these nineteenth century leaders, and they did not really follow Fundamentalism or modern Pentecostalism. Is there a theological key? I believe there is indeed a key.

Scripture is clear that upon accepting the Messiah Jesus into our lives, we have by grace been given all things in Him. We have died with Him, risen in Him, have been made partakers of His Spirit, and have ascended to the heavenlies in Him. In Him, we have all. Yet this refers to our positional standing. Theologians have long made a distinction between the positional reality of our identity in the Messiah and our practical appropriation in living out the truths of our position.

Watchman Nee wrote of the dramatic change that came with his understanding of his co-death with the Messiah. When he entered into the *full experience* of this reality he shouted, "I'm dead! Praise God!" Yet this was true before his realization. Indeed, the baptism in the Spirit could be of a similar nature. As His born-again followers, we are already *in Him*, baptized in the Spirit. Yet it is not until later that most come into the practical experience or reality of the meaning of the baptism. By faith it is appropriated.

Evangelicals and Charismatics disagree over whether or not the baptism in the Spirit occurs at conversion or in a "second blessing" experience. Parallel to the reality of our co-death with the Messiah, the answer is surely both! The experience of what is ours in the Messiah is new *to us*. The baptism *positionally* takes place at conversion. It is *appropriated* subsequently any time from minutes to years afterward, when we experience a faith-understanding and we finally take hold of what is ours.

Spiritual gifts are manifestations of this baptism. Speaking in tongues is the easiest spiritual gift to manifest, therefore tongues often accompanies the practical appropriation of the baptism in the Spirit. However, this is not always so, nor can it be *demonstrated* from Scripture. It is rather an inference from the fact of tongues accompanying the gift of the Holy Spirit in four passages in the book of Acts (Acts 2, 8, 10, and 19). We can see how the split is fostered, for some Evangelicals argue that the baptism in the Spirit is in *every sense* an accompaniment of conversion and that the gifts of the Spirit were for another age.

I began to see this as *the devil's bifurcation*. It produced two wings of the Body which greatly needed each other. One wing emphasized the objective rational interpretation of Scripture. They possessed the majority of believing scholars. The other wing produced the intuitive, spiritually sensitive, and experientially oriented leaders. Yet in the 19th century the two emphases came together even in single individuals.

In recent decades we have seen an Evangelicalism grow that is scholastic and intellectualist, along with a Pentecostalism which is subjective – as each hardens positions in reaction to the other. The anti-intellectual spiritual is opposed by the pro-intellectual anti-experiential. Yet the only thing that can bring balance is the reality of the wind of the Spirit combined with the discipline of clear thinking in handling Holy Writ.

Today, praise God, this false dichotomy is breaking down. A Pentecostal scholar, Robert Cooley, leads one of our finest seminaries (Gordon-Conwell) and Pentecostals or Charismatics are found on such faculties as Trinity and Fuller. A great Evangelical scholar, Clark Pinnock, invites fellow Evangelicals to *enter in* to the experience of the Holy Spirit and His gifts and to learn from Charismatics. Many emphasize testing the spirits and that fruit is more important than gifts. Today I lead a frankly charismatic congregation (manifesting the gifts of the Spirit). Yet I know and love the Spirit in my brethren of Presbyterian, Baptist, and other backgrounds.

In many ways, Flock Church was a tragedy born of the false division in the Body. The Body needs to present its young people with *the reality of the experience of piety* in prayer, the gifts of the Spirit, and the miracles that manifest themselves in the wind of the Spirit ... as well as the importance of in depth Scriptural study. In any unbiased reading of the New Testament, it becomes evident that a walk in the power of the Holy Spirit produces miraculous manifestations of answered prayer, healing, and supernatural gifts. This was true for a host of saintly leaders including Charles Finney, R.A. Torrey, Andrew Murray, D.L. Moody, Rees Howells, Hudson Taylor, G. Mueller, C.T. Studd, V. Raymond Edman, and many others. Likewise, the objective revelation of the Scripture for doctrine and correction should be stressed, along with the importance of humble, patient scholars. Without them we would be bereft of English translations, grammatical tools, lexicons, dictionaries, and encyclopedias. Respect for the Word and handling it carefully produces respect for the humble, pious thinker and scholar. The Evangelicals need to open up and *enter in* by faith to the fresh word of God's Spirit and His gifts, while the Charismatic needs greater concern for objective interpretation. We need to come together. Neither a cold rationalism nor an interpretive subjectivism will be adequate for a day of great spiritual deceptions by the prince of darkness. Let us not argue over words. Let us enter into the reality of spiritual life tested by the Word.

COLLEGE FACULTY

This leads to some comments concerning the dangers of Christian college education. We certainly cannot blame the college for losing its best teachers of the Word to a new and expanding seminary. Yet, it proves something crucial about the Bible and Theology college faculty. Its members must be superb in knowledge and *inspired* in teaching. They must not only have head knowledge, but be mature in spiritual experience. They serve as key models for students; their lives require elder-level maturity as in 1 Timothy 3. Teachers convey not only their head knowledge, but their lives. One of the reasons by God's grace that I was able to resist the spiritual disease of Flock was that I found such teachers! The Bible and Theology faculty therefore must reflect the greatest excellence so students will not make false judgments about the Scripture's relevance based on an uninspiring faculty.

Additionally, the rest of the faculty needs to integrate all areas of knowledge from a firm, Scriptural base. It simply will not do to teach secular psychology, literature, and science. Integration and Scriptural evaluation need to come from faculty members who also reflect a deep maturity of spiritual life and experience. The students must not simply be tossed into the deep waters of the intellectual world and told to swim. Some will swim, but too many will drown. Christian education, as well as secular education, can produce tremendous doubt and destruction if not *carefully handled*.

I have also become certain that one of the dangers to the believing student is to be wrenched out of his home congregation and to be transplanted hundreds or thousands of miles away at a college that for many replaces the local congregation. Relationship to the local congregation is not like membership in a lecture club, where one can transfer to any city and find the same lectures. Scripture teaches that a congregational relationship is like an extended family in which the members are responsible for one another for nurture and encouragement. Therefore we would question whether the Christian college can replace the student's congregation for four years.

Of course the college urges congregational attendance, but many on campus drop out since they have daily chapel and relationships with believing students. A student needs to seriously consider staying in his home congregation and building his life around this. If God leads him to a distant school, he should find a good congregation and be intimately involved as his first priority. There is reason to question the societal pattern of wrenching 17 and 18 year-olds away from a family social context in the most crucial transition period of their lives. There are enough Christian schools today that this should not be necessary.

Secondly, the Christian college should deemphasize chapel (although I have nothing against having even required chapel). The requirement of congregational attendance and service is more Scripturally sensible. The student needs the nurture of the *congregational family*. If other students and faculty attend, he will find both fellowship and commonality within the congregation. After all, if the college is really Christian, it can expect its constituents to live as Christians, which naturally implies being a *significant* part of a congregation. The Body needs to provide substantial ministry to students even if they may be only four-year members. Most crucially, pastors and teachers need to unflaggingly encourage young people in the spiritual disciplines of prayer, worship, and meditative Scripture reading. This is more important than any other discipline. They must not assume a student can apply himself to these disciplines just because he comes from a Christian background,

I believe that weaknesses in each of these areas contributed to the Flock phenomenon. However, I am delighted to say that I see great strides in Christian colleges toward correcting these deficiencies.

SUMMARY

In summary, I want to plead for Evangelicals and Charismatics to get together and find a way out of this doctrinal impasse. Their valid perspectives can be integrated. This is so desperately needed. Secondly, I want to urge that Christian colleges and the congregations together find better ways to integrate their ministries and more creatively foster the spiritual growth of their students.

CHAPTER 4

THE ISSUE OF AUTHORITY

Flock Church reflected an age in rebellion to authority. Perhaps the experience of Flock motivated me to search into the issue of authority. We live in an age of many "self-proclaimed Messiahs." All around us are men who do not come with credentials of affirmation from others to whom they are truly accountable. They set themselves up as authorities. In my view, Scripture teaches that we deeply need one another to speak into each other's lives. We never outgrow our need for the accountability that comes from relationships. Pastors need one another; leaders need one another. Sheep need shepherds. Today the Body is beset by the extremes of both authoritarianism and congregational anarchy. Balanced authority in the congregation is one of the great safeguards against destructive tendencies.

What is the nature of true authority? Authority in the Body is, of course, based on the written Word. All are responsible to understand the basics of Scripture and not to follow directions or doctrines contrary to the Word. All authority in the Body is under the authority of Jesus. Yet after making allowance for the supremacy of the Word and the fact that Scripture primarily calls us to a servant-hood instead of a position, we must admit that Scripture gives servant-leaders authority in the Body.

Servant-leaders are those who prove themselves by humility, the fruit of the Spirit, solid knowledge of the Word, and a loving care for the people of God. Servant-leaders prove themselves first by being in submission to authority. When servant-leaders are chosen of God, Scripture gives to them the role of governing in the congregations of the Messiah. They are enjoined to shepherd the flock (1 Peter 5), to teach, to admonish, to correct, and to discipline. Scripture enjoins the flock to submit to their leadership (Hebrews 13:17). This submission *never means the forfeiture of our own minds or consciences.* Nor does it mean that members of the flock cannot in an edifying way voice their disagreement. Yet ultimately the leaders set direction for the congregation. Submission implies:

1) Pulling together in unity and prayer with the direction leadership sets as long as it is not contrary to Scripture or conscience. Elder leadership also has authority to install and remove people from lesser positions.

2) Being willing to be taught and counseled by leadership; maintaining a humble and teachable attitude. Discipleship includes following the pattern of mature leaders to the degree that their pattern reflects Jesus.

3) Reserving the right of final personal decisions for oneself, though given to counsel with real listening and searching. Everyone must ultimately stand in his own conscience before God.

Leaders need to submit to a *plurality of other leaders.* Authority in the New Testament is vested in a mutually accountable *plural* leadership, though there may be a head pastor. Furthermore, we must beware of the isolated group that cuts itself off from other groups. We need brothers and sisters outside of our limited circle to interact with our lives. There is only one Church; we must see all elders as fellow leaders in the same universal Body.

Scriptural leadership is given the authority to discipline in regard to sin and serious error. This discipline begins with words of loving exhortation and correction which seeks reconciliation with the offending brother. However, if repentance is not forthcoming, it can lead to the painful discipline of disfellowshipping or excommunication. This is to hopefully turn the brother who is in gross sin back to God (1 Corinthians 5:11-13) as well as to protect the purity of the Body. The leaders must especially guard against bitterness, slander, and rebellion in its membership. These are the roots of false prophecy. Lack of discipline in many quarters in the Body is a great danger. We need to study thoroughly what Scripture says on government, authority, and discipline. One of the sad aspects of Flock was that no decision of discipline for immorality or heresy was ever given against Flock by the rest of the Body, or in regard to individual members and faculty.

Unfortunately, one of the great problems of our day is acting out of reaction. The devil's *tactic* is clear. Whenever proper Scriptural discipline and authority is invoked, cries of "Jonestown" and "Shepherding movement" resound. The devil's method is to use the extremes of cultic authority and authoritarianism to produce popular outcries which reduce leadership to impotence. Leaders give up their God-given call to hear from God, to set direction, to teach, and to discipline which thereby protects the flock. Instead they become public relations experts seeking to find ways to please all the varying sentiments of the membership. This fear on the part of leaders produces a weak congregation with poorly trained members who are pawns for aberrant movements.

Of this I am now sure: proper Scriptural authority is a bulwark against cultism and false controlling authorities. Over and over again I have seen those who rebel against proper authority become fully subject to false cultic authority. This is because rebellion, akin to witchcraft, is spiritually capable of being controlled by the devil. The solution for false cultic authority is not anarchy with the absence of authority. It is rather a return to a Scriptural teaching on the nature and place of authority and insisting on it in our congregations.

Fear of proper authority often results from wild accusations against the excesses in some parts of the "shepherding movement" and claims that we are in danger of "shepherding." *Unproven accusations* produce a reactive stance and divert us from *deeply studying the Scriptural passages that deal with the issues of conforming our lives and congregational patterns to the Word.* Thus the devil produces in the Body exactly what he desires: either false cultic authority or an anarchistic lack of authority. As people react in bitterness or slander, the prince of the air gains a victory. Let us not carry bad reports against any group unless a Matthew 18 process of discipline and evidence has been clearly followed. False movements are handled by congregational authorities, not by their absence.

What is the nature of authority? True authority seeks as its goal the maturity of the Messiah in every individual. *It seeks to facilitate in people the ability to know the Word, to pray effectively, and to manifest the gifts and fruit of the Spirit. It seeks to produce strong individuals in the LORD who are capable of spiritual discernment and solid thinking!* True submission is not dependency, but it is coordinate with the strongest self-confidence and character. False authority seeks to make people dependent on the authority. It seeks to discern and think for other people, suppressing their conscience and thinking. *The goals of true and false authority are therefore opposite and determine the patterns which are worked out in the life of the congregation.*

All men and women are forever fallible. Practical perfection, though the goal of our lives, is not to be obtained in this life. One of the pitfalls of the proud is an inability to maintain congregational commitment because servant-leaders are not deemed perfect enough. This is a dangerous stance. We can learn from anyone who loves the LORD. We can accept that God is working through any servant-leader who demonstrates a love for worshiping God, a love for the Word, and whose family life is in basic order according to 1 Timothy 3. A servant-leader who shows imperfection is to be preferred over one who has learned in pretense to project an image beyond his spiritual attainment.

All of us are called to submit to imperfect leaders. Those who admit their faults and pray for one another are to be more greatly esteemed. The quest of pride for perfect leadership, or the complaint that leaders are not adequately worthy of respect – even though they fulfill basic Scriptural criteria – is a danger signal. Such a person also may find himself attracted to a cultic leader who is full of lies and deception but has learned to *project* the image of perfection.

God has called us all to build His kingdom. In its present form, His Body is not yet perfected. We are called to live and act in love and compassionate tolerance for the benefit of all in His kingdom. With new measures of love and spiritual anointing, we are called to a task of listening and learning. Let us recognize in these last days that the devil "goes about as a roaring lion, seeking whom he may devour." Unless we draw together, seek to find Scriptural grounds for greater accord in a spirit of humility, and cease to build doctrine from reaction, the devil will have an easy time. If oppression and persecution come, the foundations must be firm, and loyalty must be instilled in the troops.

The Flock Church phenomenon touches many of the key issues in the Body today. These issues include the charismatic/non-charismatic debate, models of authority, the nature of cultic control and rebellion, the symptoms of would-be heretical groups and false authoritarianism, the educational structure for raising our children, and the authority of Scripture as an objective revelation. It is our prayer that the lessons to be learned from Flock will shed light on these issues and give direction to those in confusion.

CHAPTER 5

HELPING THE
WOUNDED

Although Scripture makes it abundantly clear that leaders bear a higher responsibility and punishment for leading people into deception, the follower still has a responsibility as well. The major issue in healing these wounded individuals is finding the roots of why the person gave himself to the deception. Our experience in providing such healing has proved to us that there is no such thing as a person being innocently deceived. The Scriptures promise that the followers of Jesus (His sheep) hear His voice, know Him, and follow Him. The roots of deception are always in pride and bitterness (unhealed hurt). This is a problem all face; therefore all are capable of being deceived. The healing process is as follows.

First, on the subject of pride, let me put forth the following. Pride is the root that causes people to buy into deceptions that they are part of *the key group being used by God*, or are part of the group that possesses *the truth in a way that is beyond all others*. This produces a heady feeling that can be mistaken for the Spirit. If this is identified as the key, then the person needs to repent of pride and admit this fault.

Secondly, on the subject of unhealed hurts, it is important to note that unhealed hurt is often bitterness. Many say, "I am not bitter – only hurt." But hurt turns to bitterness very quickly. The cure for unhealed hurt is in identifying with the death of Jesus on the cross (envisioning it, meditating on the truth of it, etc.) and coming to the place where the person can truly say of those who hurt him, "Father, forgive them, for they know not what they do." Forgiveness in this sense may not mean the restoration of the relationship, as that requires the guilty to repent and restore. However, it is a commitment to have love for the offender and to pray for his repentance and restoration to blessing. The roots of unhealed hurt are usually in the closest relationships – parents, siblings, teachers, and friends. When the wounded believer has left the cultic group, his primary bitterness will be focused on the leadership of the group. However, this usually is not the root of the problem. The person needs to see the deeper roots and confess them. Then forgiveness toward the cult leaders can follow. (Forgiveness in this sense does not mean letting them off the hook of God's righteousness or not pursuing His justice in love).

After confessing and receiving forgiveness, spiritual deliverance may be crucial. It is at least well to command any occult or other spirits of deception to be gone.

After this the person requires a period of time to build trust in true elders and deacons. The standards for leaders should be taught to the person. A Scripturally balanced knowledge of true authority and submission should be taught. Those from difficult backgrounds often trust people they should not and refuse to trust those they should. It is very important to disciple them in the Word where there is weakness, communicating how and who to trust.

The knowledge of the Word is a safeguard against deception. However, the deceived often will not honestly search the Scriptures. I have seen well-taught believers fall into deception. I have also seen new, naïve believers recognize that something is wrong with a leader or group. They seek the truth in Scripture and the counsel of others, and God gives them clarity concerning the situation.

There are many good healing resources for the unhealed hurt. There are also materials of poor quality. As a start, I would recommend Leanne Payne's *The Healing Presence*. Developing open relationships in a solid, Scripture-based community is the capstone of healing. Sometimes the person in the healing process wants to flee. Much prayer and love is sometimes needed. However, we have seen many restored to wholeness.

CHAPTER 6

THE SPIRIT OF AMERICAN RELIGIOUS LIFE

Today after over 45 years since the events of this book, I believe that we live in perilous times. Thus, there are several reasons for why the lessons of *Dynamics of Spiritual Deception* are still so important for today. When I first wrote, we had recently read of the tragedy with the Branch Davidians in Waco, Texas. They were destroyed in an explosive fire after many weeks of siege by federal agents. This cult showed how far deception can go. Today we have new strange cults, as people follow false and demonic revelations. In Israel a Korean leader has entered into relationship with Russian Jewish believers and brought them much money. He teaches that only he, uniquely, has the blood of Yeshua flowing in his veins. There are cults all over South America, and leaders of big ministries and congregations teach prosperity in a way that will mostly enrich themselves. They set up governmental structures where they are not accountable to anyone. Why does this still happen?

First is the condition of our population. With the decline of educational standards and the media's influence in building public consensus, we are in for great dangers. The Canadian philosopher Marshall McLuhan called media influence "cold communication." Truth questions are not asked, allowing an atmosphere where people do not learn how to think. The experience is all that counts. This trend is found as well in the media orientation of some mega-congregations and in television ministries. The claims and doctrine are not subject to scrutiny because, in my perception, gullibility in the Christian public is at an alarming level. This is producing a shallow, media-type spirituality. It is short on Scriptural content (keep those messages entertaining and down to 15 minutes) and very large on hype. We see this especially in the new millennials who have a humanistic concept of love that indulges sinful behavior (homosexuality and pre-marital sex), does not want to be submitted to authority in any kind of "organized religion," and finds commitment to lasting community difficult. They are open to great deception. Discipleship is at a very low ebb.

The second grave danger is the teaching that has come out of some large charismatic ministries defending the non-accountability of the head leader. He is compared to the King of Israel or to the High Priest. It is argued that he is accountable only to God. To seek to bring discipline to him through due process, as in Matthew 18, is said to be a violation of the principle to not touch God's anointed. Many such circles do not hold to 1 Timothy 3 standards for leaders. This is a dangerous situation that can lead to great disillusionment and destruction. Some in the new apostolic movements have embraced this with the non-accountable head apostle over many congregations and ministries.

The third danger is the continued growth of New Age spirituality. The ultimate prophetic direction of Flock was New Age. Granted, there are people and movements who minister prophetically being falsely accused of New Age tendencies because they pray for emotional healing and have visions. However, the number of New Agers who have significant demonic and occult abilities has increased, and they can deceive believers if they infiltrate into charismatic circles. Discernment in the Spirit and rigor with Scriptural testing for all teaching are safeguards. However, this testing must be done without a critical or paranoid spirit, which can also lead to deception. We must trust the LORD to guard His people from deception because they walk before Him in humility and forgiveness.

One of the keys to avoiding the deceptions that arise from these dangers is utilizing a quality discipleship program through small groups overseen by truly accountable and healthy leaders. The elders can be accountable to each other and to leaders outside of the local structure. It is important for congregations to not be sectarian in separateness from others. People need to ask serious questions about accountability, doctrine, and structure. (Our book *Due Process* deals with many of these issues.) Discipleship must deal with character building in the context of solid Scriptural teaching. Character is built in service. Actually, those who are prone to deception will likely be deceived, and those prone to lead in unhealthy ways will likely do so. What is the solution? It is for those who see the issues and who are spiritually healthy to raise up disciples so more and more of the people of God will be healthy. Healthy believers of character, true doctrine, and spiritual anointing will not be prone to deception.

A NOTE ON WOMEN IN LEADERSHIP

I would not be true to my own convictions if in dealing with the issue of deception, I did not speak of the issue of women in leadership. It is my conviction, despite much debate among Evangelicals, that God has established a distinction of roles for men and women and that this distinction of roles is to be reflected both in the family and the congregation. One of the sources of community deception is often to be found in women assuming roles that are not proper both in the home and the congregation. Another such source of deception is male congregational leadership representing a home that is not in right spiritual order according to 1 Timothy 3.

Having said all concerning mutual submission, love and selflessness, the fifth chapter of Ephesians clearly teaches that the husband has authority in the home. The general is not better than the corporal, but he has greater authority. So the husband is called to imitate the Messiah in his authority in the home. The proper, loving exercise of this authority in an orderly home is a key criteria for eldership in 1 Timothy 3. The structure of authority in the Body therefore is built upon the structure of the home. It enhances, complements, and reflects the home. To reverse authority in the Body, whereby the wife would be an elder over her husband, would have been unthinkable to the apostles.

Is there a reason for this role distinction beyond the value of teaching children to learn from role distinctions in their authority relationships? Yes, there is, and it is connected with the issue of deception. A man who rules his home well is less likely to fall to deception. He is secure as an individual. In 1 Timothy 2:11-14, Paul gives a further reason connected to deception. This passage is often misunderstood. Paul is teaching that a woman should not teach or have authority over a man. I take this to mean teaching in contexts and content which would give her governmental authority over men. Paul then gives us his reason, the structure of the creation order. Adam was formed, then Eve. In the Genesis account this is expanded to show that Eve was given to Adam as his helper and partner. Authority vested in the man is as old as creation. It is not a result of the fall, although the wrong exercise of that authority is a result of the fall. Finally, Paul argues, the woman was first deceived. What is the point of this being included in the argument? Women, called the weaker vessel in Scripture, are weaker only in some regards. She is first deceived because of this weakness. Here Paul is speaking of a general principle, not true of each and every woman. It is woman's greater sensitivity to the intuitive and spiritual. Hence we find that the devil chooses to tempt through the woman. Women in general are more sensitive to spiritual things; they make up a larger percentage of most congregations. Yet this sensitivity predisposes them to spiritual influences both good and evil. Men, with more of a tendency to question, are often slower to receive spiritual promptings but less apt to fall into deception. Hence, governmental authority and protection for the flock is given to men who prove themselves in family leadership. Does this mean that men may not be as spiritually sensitive and deceived at times?

No, it does not. Nor does it mean that a woman may not develop a high ability of testing. It simply means that the tendency in general of the sexes is to be reflected positively in roles, and in the training of men and women for their respective roles, in the home and the congregation. This works against the dangers of deception although it does not preclude it. Men who are proven in their families, Scripturally trained, and who love the flock are a bulwark against deception.

Printed in the United States
By Bookmasters